FAMILY GAMES NIGHT

Introduction

Welcome to your ultimate companion for a fun night at home with the family!

There really is no better way to bond and build memories as a family than with play and games. Play has been proven to strengthen relations, relieve stress and improve language and motor neuron skills (in all ages!)

Family Games Night is packed to the rim with games, challenges, quizzes and conversation starters. All the games are easy to set up and quick to learn, replacing the traditional board games with active, silly and hands-on games. They are fun for all ages; children (from age six up), teens and adults.

I've had a lot of fun compiling these over the last year and have tried them all out on my own family. It's been a great excuse to ditch the screens in exchange for fun and laughter, and game nights are now a regular in our household.

The games, activities and challenges are all organised at random to encourage you to try something new. You can work your way through the book in order. Or get your kids to flick through and pick a page that takes their fancy.

Let the competitions begin........!

A note on adapting games...

Games are only fun if everyone feels they have a fair chance at winning. They have to be attainable otherwise the player can feel frustrated and, worse, it can even knock their confidence.

With this in mind, you should adapt some of the games to make them fair if you have younger players in your family. This could be making older players play with one hand or giving younger members additional time.

QUICK CHANGE

You'll need: No equipment needed

Choose someone to start the game. They stand in the middle of the room and do a full circle.

Next, they leave the room and, in secret, change something about their appearance. It could be folding down a cuff, taking an earring out or undoing a button.

The person returns to the room and does another circle. The first player to call out what has changed is next to be on.

When appearances become too easy, you can switch to items in the room. All players close their eyes, and while their eyes are closed, the player who is on changes something in the room.

INSIDE OUTSIDE

Mark a circle on the floor (using rope or printer's tape) big enough for everyone to stand in.

Someone is the Umpire and calls 'in' or 'out' in whatever order they like. For example: 'in, in, out, in, out, out, out'.

When the Umpire says 'in', everyone must jump so they are in the circle, and vice versa when the Umpire says 'out'. Players' feet must stay together at all times, and other than jumping, they can't move.

If someone gets it wrong, hesitates, or takes a step, then they are out of the game. Keep playing until you have the winner - they become the next Umpire.

If you want to make the game more challenging, you can then swap commands, so out means in and in means out!

Equipment: None

Three people take part: one is the boss, one is the employee who has arrived late to work, and one is the co-worker. The boss stands facing the employee, while the co-worker stands behind the boss, so the employee can see the co-worker, but the boss cannot.

The boss begins by sternly asking the employee, "Why are you late?" The employee starts giving an excuse, but it must describe what the co-worker is silently miming behind the boss.

The co-worker might mime things like marching, dancing, swatting at flies, being attacked, or wrestling an imaginary animal. The employee must build a believable (or at least entertaining) excuse based on whatever the co-worker is doing. At any moment, the boss can suddenly turn around, catch the co-worker in the act, and demand, "What are you doing?!" The co-worker must immediately come up with a sensible, office-appropriate explanation that matches their miming.

For example, if they were pretending to fight a bear, they might say, "Oh, I was just trying to open this stubborn pastry bag — thanks for the crullers, boss!"

If the boss buys the excuse, they say "Okay," and the game continues. If the excuse isn't convincing (or just doesn't amuse the boss), the boss shouts "You're fired!" and a new player becomes the co-worker.

WHAT'S YOUR excuse?

MASTER & SERVENT

You'll need: No equipment needed

This is a role-play storytelling game. One person gives orders, the Master, and the other person explains why he can't carry them out, the Servant. The answer has to be part of a consistent narrative.

For example:

Master: Fetch me a coffee
Servent: I would, but I just broke my foot
Master: Then order me a coffee on Uber Eats
Servant: I would, but I broke my foot when I fell over, and at the same time, it smashed my phone
Master: Well, use my phone then
Servant: I would but now I think about it I might've hit my head at the same time and I've forgotten how to use a phone

And so on......

ACTIVITY IDEA

READY, STEADY, COOK

Head to the supermarket together. Everyone selects 5 of their favourite raw ingredients.

At home, see if you can come up with some fun meal ideas using the ingredients you bought

The one rule.... no looking up recipes on your phone!

Equipment: Plastic cups

This is a 2 player game. Take turns to play.

On a table, line up half the plastic cups, face down, next to each other in a line. Do the same on the other side of the table for the exact same number of cups. At the end of the table is a bin (you may want to put a clean bin bag in so the cups don't get dirty).

Player 1 stands on one side of the table and Player 2 on the other. On 'go,' both players move the cups into the bin. They can only touch one cup at a time and need to decide what tactics to use; ie, what order to do this in.

The first player to clear their line of cups wins.

Bin the Cups

Would you rather be able to fly or be invisible?

....

Would you rather always have to sing everything you say or dance everywhere you go?

....

Would you rather only be able to communicate by texting or never use technology to communicate again?

....

Would you rather have one wish granted today or three wishes granted in 10 years? (what would those wishes be?)

Conversation Prompts

How well do you know each other? Test each other out with these questions - whoever answers has to give a reason why!

FAMILY JUDO

Take turns to compete with each other two at a time. Keep playing until everyone has had a turn and you have your ultimate Judo Champion!

The first two to compete stand facing each other, chest to chest and feet shoulder width apart. Take a step back so they're about a metre apart.

They raise their hands, palms outward, pressing them against their partner's hands. The goal is to make your opponent lose their balance and move their feet, but you can only achieve this by pushing against each other's hands - you can't grab, pull or touch any other body part.

Players improve after each game, so play a couple of rounds. If one player has a distinct advantage (ie, they are bigger), you can make it more of an even playing field by having their feet together, making it harder for them to keep balance.

A man was driving a black truck. His lights were not on. The moon was not out. A lady was crossing the street.

How did the man see her?

Answer: It was a bright, sunny day

ACTIVITY IDEA

INDOOR CAMPING

Use blankets, pillows, and furniture to create a cozy den in the living room.

You can use it to watch a film or even bring your duvets and sleep there together overnight.

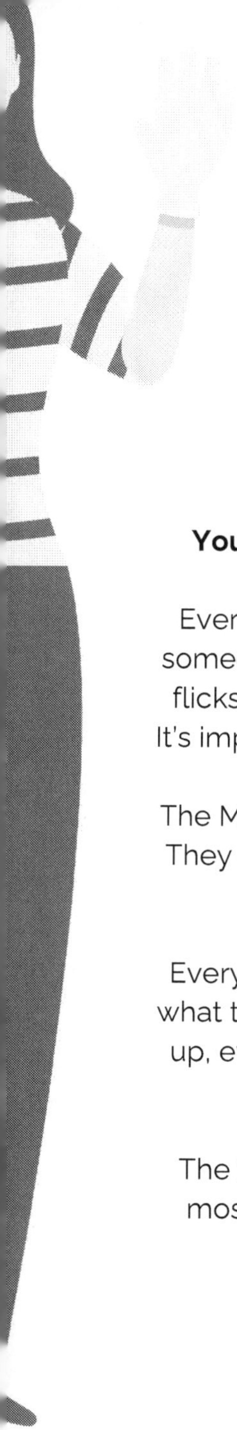

GAME: MIME ARTIST

You'll need: Pen and paper, family photo album

Everyone needs a pen and paper to hand. Choose someone to be the first 'mime artist'. The Mime Artist flicks through a family album and chooses a photo. It's important that no one else sees the chosen photo.

The Mime Artist has 5 minutes to describe the photo. They can't speak or use sounds, but they can mime, point and act.

Everyone else draws, in as much detail as possible, what they think is being described. Once 5 minutes is up, everyone shows their drawings and the original photo is revealed.

The Mime Artist chooses who they think drew the most accurate picture, and that person is next to choose and mime a photo.

HIM OR HER

You'll need: Prepare a deck of questions in advance

Divide players up into pairs (it's up to you how you split, ie you could do grown-ups against children or have one of each in a team).

The first team to play are asked a question from the deck, such as 'who is the fastest runner'. The answer will be one of the team members' names, so if Dad and his son Steve are playing, the answer will either be 'Dad' or 'Steve'.

Both members have to guess how their teammate will answer that question. They can either write the name down or be back-to-back with each other and hold up something that indicates their answer (i.e., they both have a wooden spoon and a flashlight, and the wooden spoon represents Dad and the flashlight Steve).

If they both get the same answer, they get a point. Now switch so the other team answers. At the end of the game, tally the scores.

Ideas for questions (get everyone involved in writing out the deck of cards and coming up with their own ideas):
Whose music taste is better?
Who is the clumsiest?
Who can eat the most?
Who has a better sense of style?
Who spends more time on their phone?
Who has the best-looking friends?
Who is more likely to be late for a date?
Who is more likely to cry during a sad film?

Tell me about...

Think you know each other well? Take turns asking each other (including the grown ups) the following questions...you might be surprised what you find out!

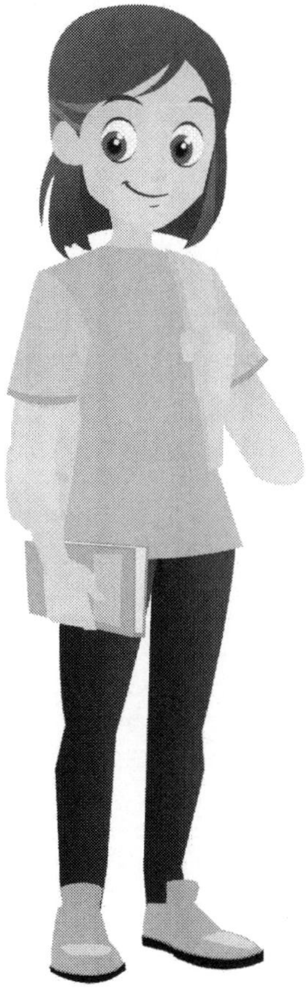

...a time when you were really proud of yourself!

...the most interesting person you've ever met!

...your dream job!

...the best vacation you've ever taken!

...something that always makes you happy!

....something you'd love to learn!

....a time you took a risk and it paid off!

...a time you helped someone!

FICTIONARY

Equipment: Dictionary and slips of paper

This is a nice game to play at the dinner table, especially for families with older children. Choose a player to be 'on'. Using a dictionary, they choose an obscure word no one knows and read it aloud. The player who is 'on' writes down the correct definition on a slip while everyone else invents a fake one. "On" then reads all the definitions aloud, and the other players must guess which one is real.

After everyone has made their guesses, the real definition is revealed. Players earn points in a few different ways: by correctly identifying the real definition, by fooling others into choosing their fake one. A new player is 'on' for the next round.

There are ground rules: no proper nouns, acronyms, abbreviations, or words from foreign languages. Players can't vote for their own definitions, and the person's on' doesn't vote at all. Adults should vote last to avoid swaying the others.

Equipment: Long or rocket balloons

This is a simple and silly game that will have you all laughing. You'll need one balloon for each player. Each balloon needs to be a different colour so they can identify which is theirs.

Blow up the balloons so they are all the same size. Instead of tying them off, have each player hold the end.

Everyone stands facing each other, holding their balloon pointing upwards. On a command, everyone lets go of their balloons at the same time. The aim of the game is to catch your balloon before it hits the ground.

Catch the Balloon

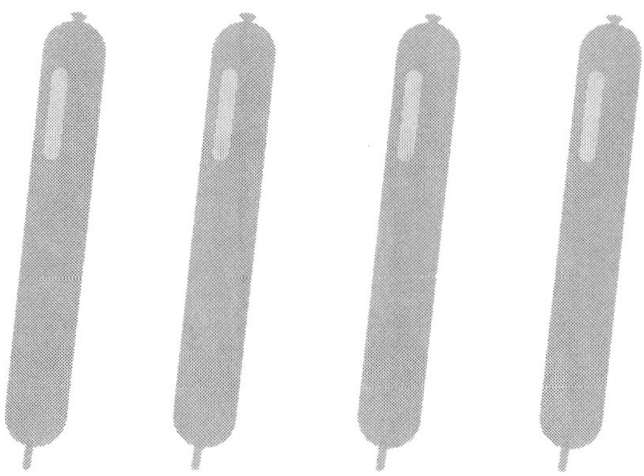

ACTIVITY IDEA

NIGHT HIKE

Get everyone into their pyjamas early, and instead of your usual bedtime routine, put on jackets and head outside. Going on a night hike as a family is a really fun activity. Kids will love having a flashlight, but make sure you also turn them off at some point, though, and spend some time in silence listening to the sounds of the night.

TOP TIP: Pick up a UV flashlight from a second-hand site and head to the woods or beach. Search out bioluminescence in fungi and insects living on the trees, or creatures living in rockpools.

CUP ON THE HEAD

Everyone starts by standing away from each other. Each player balances a plastic cup on their head (have the cup rim side down for kids and up for adults).

On 'go', everyone must try to knock the cups off the heads of other players while also ensuring their own stays balanced.

The last person with a cup still on their head wins.

GAME: NINJA

You'll need: No equipment needed

Everyone starts in a circle close together. On three, everyone jumps back from the circle and adopts a ninja pose. They must be frozen and can't move until they hear 'ninja'.

Going around the circle, take turns. Player one shouts 'ninja'. When they do this, they do a single step and movement. The movement must be decisive and fluid, like a clear karate chop. The person who is playing is aiming to do a move that results in them hitting another player in the arm or hand. If they succeed, that player is out.

When the players hear 'ninja', they have an option to do a counter move to avoid being hit (this is not compulsory, only if they think they might be targeted). If they decide to do a counter move, this also can only consist of a single step and a decisive, fluid movement. There is some guesswork here as they don't know what move their opponent will make.

Go around the circle, taking turns shouting 'ninja' and doing an attacker move.

If you are touched on the arm or hand by an attacker, you are out of the game. Keep playing until there's one player left, the winner.

Would you rather always have to wear wet socks or always wear shoes that are one size too small?

....

Would you rather be the funniest person in the room or the smartest person in the room?

....

Would you rather travel the world but never be able to return to your home country, or never leave your home country again?

....

Would you rather have to always have to tell the truth or have everyone else alway tell you the truth?

Conversation Prompts

How well do you know each other? Test each other out with these questions - whoever answers has to give a reason why!

SOCKS

Create a space so that everyone can lie on the floor. Everyone must wear a pair of socks.

Challenge one is to be the first to remove your socks without using your hands!

Challenge two is to remove everyone else's socks while keeping yours on. The last person with a sock on is the winner!

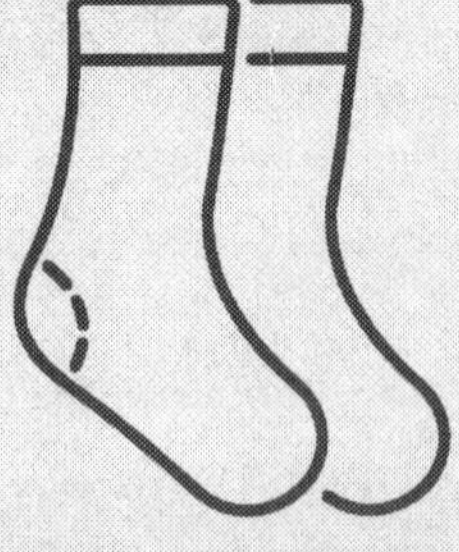

ACTIVITY IDEA

THE FLOOR IS LAVA

Create an elaborate obstacle course in your house using chairs, cushions, tables and anything else you are happy for everyone to climb on.

Now see if everyone can get themselves from A to B without touching the floor, AKA the lava! If someone touches the floor, they have to go back to the start.

You can make the game extra fun by continuing the obstacle course up the stairs and between different rooms, or each family member creates their own obstacle course in a different room before connecting them to make one long challenge.

GUIDED MISSILES

You'll need: A piece of string and two blindfolds

You'll need four players for this game, but you can rotate if you have extra players.

Two of the players will missles and will be blindfolded and placed standing next to each other. Each missile has a commander, the other person on the team. Commanders stand on the other side of the room.

After the missiles have been blindfolded, place a piece of string on the floor in a circle shape (big enough for someone to stand fully in it). This is the planet that the missiles are aiming to get to.

Each commander takes turns giving their missile instructions. This consists of a direction followed by a number of steps, but nothing more, ie, 'turn left and take two big steps.'

Alternate giving instructions. The first missile to have their feet fully inside the circle is the winner!

FAMILY CHARADES

You'll need: No equipment needed

A fun twist on a classic. A family member stands up and silently acts out a shared memory using only mime (no talking, sounds or pointing allowed). The shared memory could be a party that you had together, a funny moment on vacation or a wedding you attended. The only rule is that everyone had to have been there.

Whoever guesses correctly first is next to stand up and mime a new memory.

SKITTLES

You'll need: Large bag of skittles (can also use small marshmallows or Malteasers instead), staws and plates

Each player sits around the table with a plate in front of them and a straw in hand.

In the middle, scatter the bag of Skittles.

On 'go' players must put as many of the skittles on their plate until there are none left on the table. They can only move one skittle at a time and can only use the straw. They do this by placing one end of the straw on the skittle and sucking on the other end.

Once all the skittles have been collected, count how many each player has on their plate to work out the winner.

ACTIVITY IDEA

BOOK NIGHT

A twist on the classic family film night.

Instead of a film, you read a book together, taking it in turns to read a chapter aloud.

Just like a film night, you can make the space cozy, have everyone in their pyjamas early and put out a spread of delicious snacks.

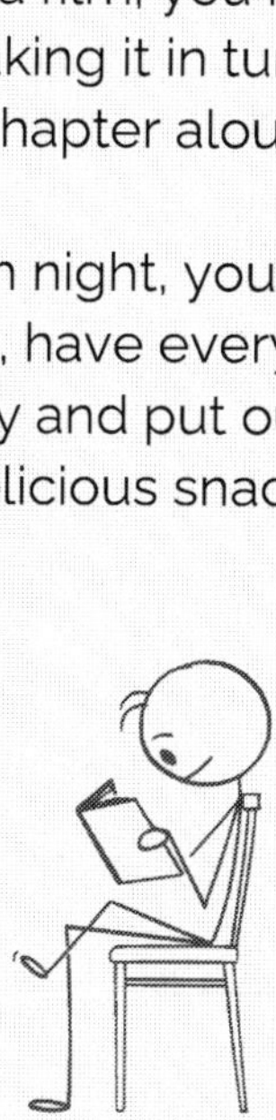

SARDINES

You'll need: No equipment needed, although this does need to be played in the dark

This game is a fun take on hide and seek. First, go around the house and turn off all the lights and draw the curtains so it's as dark as possible. Also, put away anything that might be dangerous or break if knocked....like your favourite vase!

Everyone starts in the smallest room with the lights on - I also like to play music here, so you can't try to cheat and listen to where the hider is going. One person leaves (they can take a torch if they like) and is given a few minutes to head off into the dark house to find a hiding spot.

The rest of the players leave the small room one at a time, and a few minutes apart. They must move around the house in the dark using their hands to try to find the hidden person.

When they find them, they must quietly join them - hence the name sardines. If there's someone else in the room with you at the time, don't react if you find the hider, but instead wait until you are on your own to join them.

The last person left at the end loses and is the next to go hide!

GLUED

Someone sits in a chair and tilts their head backwards so they are looking up at the ceiling. Another person stands behind them and places their little finger on the person's forehead.

Instruct the person sitting down to stand up while the other person uses their little finger to stop them. They'll find it's surprisingly difficult.

Take turns so everyone has a go!

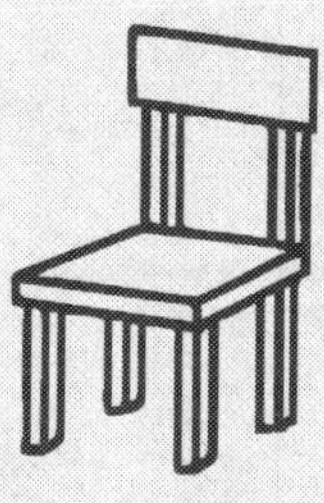

Would you rather live without your favorite food forever or live without any screens for a year?

....

Would you rather have the ability to time travel to the past or see into the future?

....

Would you rather be stuck on a deserted island alone or with someone who really annoys you?

....

Would you rather have feet instead of hand or hands instead of feet?

....

Would you rather have a personal driver or a personal chef?

Conversation Prompts

How well do you know each other? Test each other out with these questions - whoever answers has to give a reason why!

A doctor and a boy were fishing. The boy was the doctor's son, but the doctor was not the boy's father.

Who was the doctor?

Answer: His mother

NEWSPAPER CHALLENGE

You'll need two old newspapers.

Split into two teams. Each team must choose someone whom they will dress up using only the newspaper.

Once a set time is up, have the models do a catwalk showcasing their new outfits.

Next, have the two teams dress a new member up as a mummy using just the newspaper!

ACTIVITY IDEA

FACNY NIGHT IN

Who says you need to go out to dress up?

Create a fancy night in. Have the kids design an invite or poster for the night. Everyone dresses up in their fanciest outfits.

Have a posh sit-down meal with all your favourite food. Then, how about a dance party afterwards in the living room with everyone's favourite track?

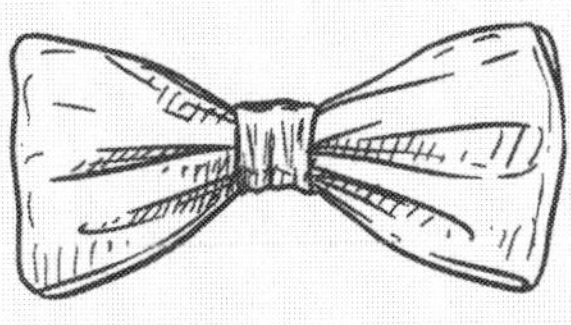

Almost everyone needs it, asks for it, and gives it, but almost nobody takes it.

What is it?

Answer: Advice

BLIND TASTE TEST

Start the challenge with the grown-ups blindfolded. The kids must choose ten items of food from the kitchen and feed them to the grown-ups with a spoon. The grown-ups get a point for each food item they correctly guess.

Now switch and have the children blindfolded and guessing the food that the grown-ups feed them.

You might want to hide the hot sauce for this game!

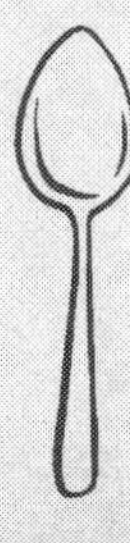

FRUIT FRUIT FRUIT

You'll need: No equipment needed

To start the game, everyone chooses a fruit; for example, Dad might decide he's an Orange.

Decide who will kick off the game. At any time, that person can try to get out another player by saying their fruit three times in a row. So, let's say they wanted to get out Dad, they'd say "Orange, orange, orange".

To stop himself from being out, Dad needs to say his fruit once in full, "Orange", before the person 'on' has said it three times. If he succeeds in saying it fast enough, the person who started remains so. If not, then Dad is now on and must choose who to get out next.

This game works well if you play it on-going throughout the night so you can try and catch people out when they are distracted or not expecting it.

ACTIVITY IDEA

HOUSE OLYMPICS

Every family member has to design a home Olympic sport. This could be an obstacle course, a staring or balancing competition or a game of Scrabble.

Either work in teams or as individuals. Throughout the night, play each of the Olympic sports, keeping track of winners.

Have an award ceremony at the end of the night. You can get the kids to make trophies or medals in advance for the winners.

ROCK, PAPER, SISSORS, *SPLITS*

You'll need: No equipment needed

A classic game of Rock, Paper and Scissors but with a twist! The first two components stand facing each other. One foot will be facing forward, and the other will be directly behind that foot, so the toe is touching the heel.

Someone will be on hand to be the judge, and they will call out 'Rock, paper, scissors, go'. On 'go', both competing players do the usual hand action to indicate if they've chosen rock, paper or scissors.

Whoever wins the round must move the foot that is behind back a foot length, so their feet are moving slowly into the position of the splits.

Keep playing until a player falls or can no longer hold the splits. The winner stays on and plays a new opponent. Keep going until everyone has played and you have your champion!

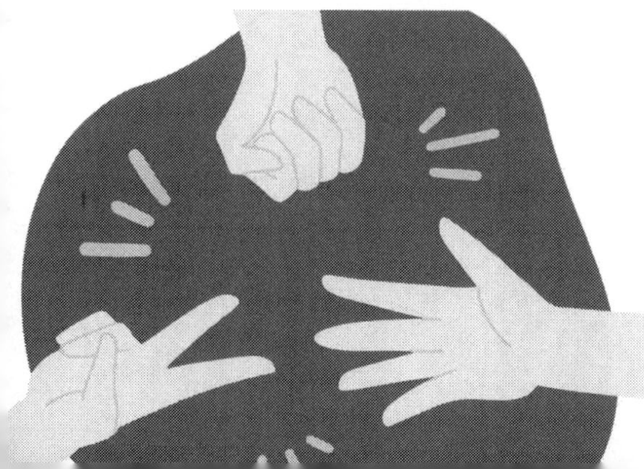

YES

Choose someone to be 'on'.

Everyone else has 5 minutes to try anything they can to get that person to say 'yes'. The only rule is that the person who is 'on' must answer any question that someone asks them (they can't just refuse to speak).

Once the time is up, choose a new player to be 'on'.

What has 13 hearts...

...but no other organs?

Answer: A deck of playing cards

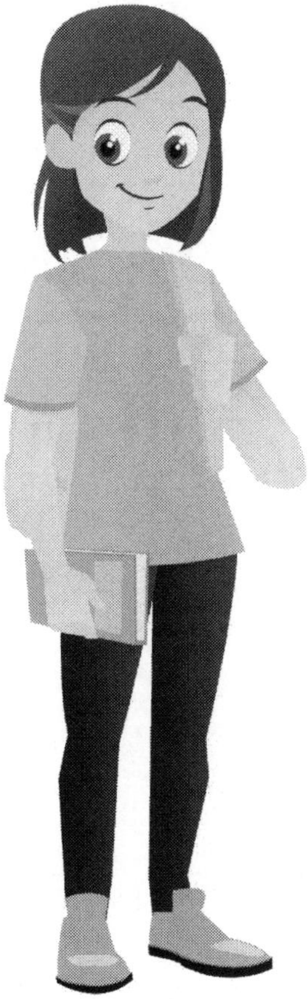

What would you do...

Think you know each other well? Take turns asking each other (including the grown ups) the following questions...you might be surprised what you find out!

...if you won the lottery tomorrow?

...you had to spend a year living in a different country?

....you had to dedicate a year to learning a new sport or musical instrument?

...you could have any super power of your choosing?

....you had to start a new business?

...you were president for a week?

....had unlimited funds to organise the vacation of your dreams?

MATCHBOX

You'll need 2 old matchboxes or boxes of a similar size.

Split into 2 teams, each is given a box. You have 10 minutes to fill your matchbox with as many items as you can fit.

Once the time is up, come together to count the items and see who has the most!

PTERODACTYL

You'll need: No equipment needed

Sit in a circle so you can all see each other. Everyone needs to cover their teeth with their mouths so they aren't showing (think mimicking someone who has lost their teeth). Player one starts by turning to their left and saying 'pterodactyl'. They must keep their teeth covered at all times.

Continue in this manner clockwise. At any point, a player can change the direction of play by turning back to the player who has just said 'pterodactyl', screeching and flapping their arms. All this needs to happen with teeth still hidden!

The player receiving the screech can either continue with the new direction or screech back to change the direction again. And so on...

A player is out if they show their teeth at any point. This becomes nearly impossible when the laughter starts!

Would you rather be trapped in a room full of spiders or a room full of snakes?

Would you rather live in a world with no music or a world with no movies?

Would you rather have an unlimited amount of money or unlimited time?

Would you rather be able to read minds or be invisible?

Would you rather spend a year living in a 5-star all-inclusive resort or a cabin in the wilderness?

Conversation Prompts

How well do you know each other? Test each other out with these questions - whoever answers has to give a reason why!

ONE WORD STORY

Someone starts the story with a generic word, for example, “I” or“the.”

The next player will then say the next word, it can be any word at all as long as it makes sense in a sentence when added to the previous word/s.

The story continues with each player adding one word at a time. See what weird and wonderful story comes out!

ACTIVITY IDEA

TIME CAPSULE

Creating a time capsule is a really fun activity to do as a family.

You'll need a box (maybe something the kids can also decorate as part of the challenge). Now everyone must choose an item to put in the capsule. It's also nice to write letters to each other. Include predictions of what you think you'll be doing in the future.

Now seal the box and put it somewhere safe with a 'to open' date on the lid. Aim to open the box in five years' time, when you can have another special family night rummaging through the box and having a laugh as you read out everyone's predictions.

PICTIONARY

You'll need: Create cards in advance with household items on them, plus large pieces of paper or a whiteboard

Split into two teams. Pick a player from the first team to stand up and pick a card (make sure no one else sees the word). They have one minute to draw the word for their team - they can't speak, point or use letters. Someone on the other team keeps track of the timer.

If someone on team one guesses correctly within a minute, they get a point; if not, then no points. Now the other team has a go. Keep taking turns until you've had enough.

Keep track of scores to see which team wins.

Shoe SHUFFLE

You'll need: No equipment needed

This is a silly but fun game which is just as enjoyable to watch as to join in.

Everyone brings a pair of their shoes. Stand in a circle, blindfolded. One person will sit out of the game and is responsible for taking everyone's shoes and mixing them up in the middle - it's fine to throw a couple of bogus pairs in there, too.

On 'go', everyone who is blindfolded must make their way to the pile and try to work out which pair is there's using touch (and smell?) alone. The first person to put on their pair of shoes wins and sits out of the next round.

You can make the rounds harder by also including other items of clothing such as hats, gloves or coats.

WHO AM I

You'll need: Post-it notes

Start by choosing a category. It could be famous celebrities, book characters or items you'll find in the kitchen.

Sit in a circle or around a table. The person to your right chooses a person or object and writes it (secretly) on a post-it note, then fixes it to your forehead in a way that you can't see what's on there.

Once everyone has a Post-it note on their forehead, take turns going around the circle. When it's your turn, you can ask a question to try and determine what's on your post-it note. It must be a 'yes' or 'no' question, such as, am I a boy? Am I a hard object? Do I have brown hair?

The rest of the players must answer the question.

A player can make a guess as to their person or object at any time, but can only have one guess per round. See who is quickest to work it out!

COOKIE ON THE FACE

Everyone is giving a cookie (don't eat it...yet!)

On 'go', everyone tilts their head back and puts their cookie on their forehead. They must try to get the cookie in their mouth without using their hands.

If it falls on the floor, it is picked up and starts back on the forehead again.

First to get the cookie in their mouth wins!

JELLY BEAN BUMBLE

You'll need: Jelly beans and a paper bag

Everyone sits around the table. In the middle have a paper bag filled with jelly beans.

Everyone pulls four jelly beans out of a bag. Players can look at their jelly beans but will want to do it in a way that keeps it hidden from others.

On the count of three, everyone passes one jelly bean of their choosing to the left. If at any point a player gets a set of three jelly beans, they put them out in front of them in a group and then replace them with the same number of jelly beans from the bag.

Once players have put down any sets, you count to three and do the same again.

The first player to get three sets of three is the winner!

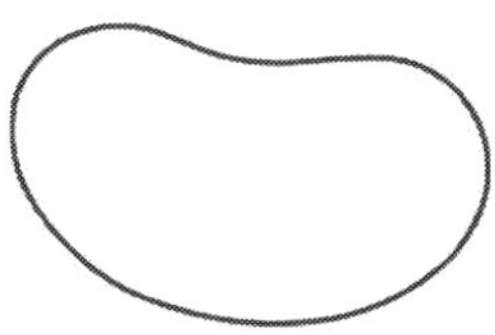

A man and a dog were going down the street. The man rode, yet walked.

What was the dog's name?

Answer: Yet

ACTIVITY IDEA

'YES' NIGHT

You might not love it.....but the kids will!!

Have a night (or a day if you're feeling brave!) where the kids are in control.

The rule is that you have to say 'yes' to whatever the kids say they want to do.

It's a good idea to set boundaries before you start playing such as, it can't cost more than X amount, it can't be dangerous and has to be within 20 minutes of home.

Good luck!

VEGGIE *JUMBLE*

You'll need: Mix of vegetables and bowls

This is best played with 2 players at a time. Players are blindfolded and stand in front of a table. Each player is given a bowl to hold

Vegetables are placed at random in front of the players. Someone who is not playing is the referee and calls out the name of a vegetable, such as 'carrot'.

The blindfolded players must use their free hand to find and guess where the carrot is. Once they think they have i,t they put it in their bowl. If they guess correctly, the referee takes the vegetable and puts it in the other player's bowl.

Keep playing until all the vegetables are off the table. The player with the most in their bowl wins.

You can mix up this game by adding in fruits or playing it with household items instead.

CHUBBY BUNNY

You'll need: Marshmallows

Someone starts the game by putting a marshmallow in their mouth and saying the words "chubby bunny" without the marshmallow falling out.

The next player does the same, and the next, and so on, until everyone has one marshmallow in their mouth.

Now for round two: put a second marshmallow in your mouth and say "chubby bunny". Keep adding marshmallows each round.

If someone can no longer say the words, or marshmallows fall out when they do, they are out of the game. See who can go the longest.

You'll need: No equipment needed

One person starts by quietly thinking of an adverb. Other players have to guess what the adverb is. They do this by setting them a task, such as 'making a cake' or 'going for a walk'.

The player who is 'on' must act out this task in the manner of their adverb. So if they are thinking of 'angrily', then they will make a cake or go for a walk with anger. They can use words, actions and noises but can't describe or use the word in question.

If a player thinks they know the answer, they shout it out. When someone guesses correctly, they are next to be 'on'.

In the Manner

STACKING CUPS

You'll need 10 plastic cups and 2 pieces of string tied in a loop.

The first 2 people to compete stand at the end of the table. Lay out 5 plastic cups in front of each person and give them the string.

Using just the string, the player must stack the cups. They do this by putting the loop around the cup and twisting it in opposite directions until it's tight around the cup, and they can lift it up.

The fastest player to stack all their cups wins and competes against the next player.

Tell me about...

Think you know each other well? Take turns asking each other (including the grown ups) the following questions...you might be surprised what you find out!

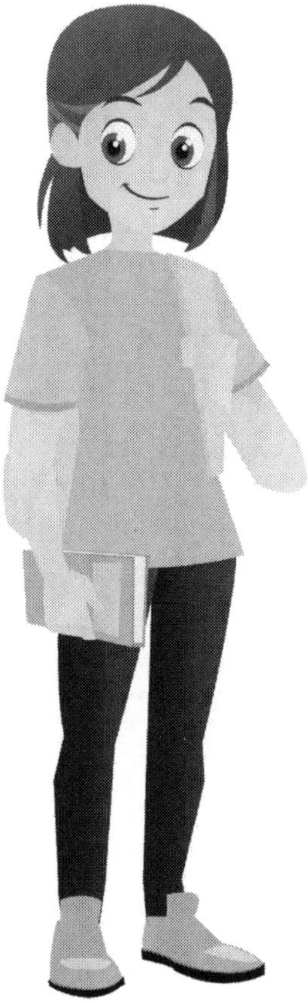

....your favorite childhood memory!

....a place you would really love to visit!

....the most important lesson you've learned in life so far!

...the biggest challenge you've faced and how you overcame it.

...your favorite book or film and why it's so special to you!

...the most adventurous thing you've ever done!

...your biggest goal in life!

COLOURS

You'll need to lots different coloured pens and a long piece of paper. Write a list of colours where the words and colour of pen don't match. For example, it might say:

PINK (written in blue pen)
YELLOW (written in orange pen)
GREY (written in black pen)
BLUE (written in red pen)
and so on.....

Players take turns reading the list but must say the colour it is, not the word that is written. It's difficult!

If they make a mistake, a new player gets to have a go.

I'D JUST LIKE TO SAY........

Thank you for picking up a copy of *Family Games Night* and making it to the end.

I tested every single activity and game out with my own family. It was great fun and helped strengthen our bond.....I really hope that's a gift that I am passing on to you!

It wasn't always easy, though. As any parent will know, it's a serious juggle managing any passion project alongside looking after small humans. But it has been worth the effort. Not just for the fun and games, but also because my children saw their mum pursuing her dream of being an author.

Before I leave you, I have a small (but very important!) favour to ask. As a teeny-tiny independent author, one of the biggest factors in how successful my book will be is the number of reviews I have.

It's mad, but true!

I'd therefore be *incredibly* grateful if you could take a minute, **right this moment**, and head to Amazon to leave this book a short review. I know you are busy and have a million things to do, so for anyone who does this, I want to say the biggest thank you!!

Please don't forget to also check out the other books in my series. If you love playing games, I've got you covered!! There's a reason my friends call me the 'games master'. I've published Party Games for Adults, Games for Teens, Games for Couples and more :)

Other books in the Games series....

And so many more!!

Printed in Dunstable, United Kingdom

70064714R00036